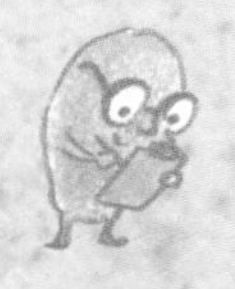

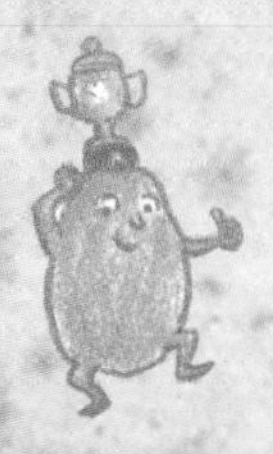

to Jane Tubb and all other chocoholics – **P.H.**

First published 2007 by Walker Books Ltd, 87 Vauxhall Walk, London SE11 5HJ

10 9 8 7 6 5 4 3 2 1

This book has been typeset in Golden Cockerel ITC and Woodland ITC

Printed in China

British Library Cataloguing in Publication Data:
a catalogue record for this book is available from the British Library
ISBN 978-1-84428-752-9

www.walkerbooks.co.uk

Chocolate

THE BEAN THAT CONQUERED THE WORLD

VIVIAN FRENCH

illustrated by PAUL HOWARD

WALKER BOOKS
AND SUBSIDIARIES
LONDON • BOSTON • SYDNEY • AUCKLAND

CONTENTS

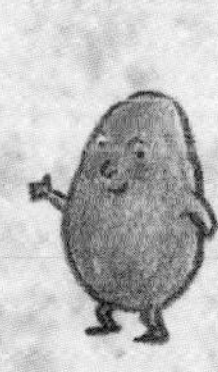

INTRODUCTION

Please read these words out loud.

Chocolate... **CHOCOLATE**... *Chocolate*...

And now check the result. Did your tongue positively curl round the word chocolate? Did your brain send up an immediate passionate longing for chocolate? Are you thinking at this exact moment of that wonderful feeling when chocolate begins to melt into a smooth, velvety softness in your mouth? If any of the above reactions are true of you, then you are one of the millions and millions of chocoholics in this world, and this book is dedicated to you.

My childhood was punctuated by the joy of chocolate. Chocolate bars, chocolate biscuits, and hot chocolate to drink on cold frosty days. Mmmm! It was only when I grew up that I discovered that chocolate had been around for literally thousands of years, and that for most of that time it was a DRINK, not a bar. Then someone told me it wasn't a drink like the hot chocolate I still have at bedtime. That's made from cocoa powder, they said – not the whole bean.

I didn't know what they meant, so I decided to find out. A chocolate bean? It sounded MAGIC! But where did this bean grow? I first met it in the tropical rainforests, but then I followed it on a journey that took me through history and across continents. I learned about geography, cooking, slavery, technology, biology AND chemistry along the way. But there was one thing nobody could tell me – how it all began. However hard I looked, I couldn't find out who was the very first person to discover that cocoa beans made chocolate. So I made up a story, and it could, just could, be true...

How the Bean Became a Drink: A STORY

THE canopy of trees in the lowlands of the Gulf Coast of Mexico boasts as many colours of green as the swelling and rolling sea. The giants stand high, thrusting branches up into the searing heat of the sun, while below, the shyer and smaller trees are happy to take advantage of the shade. The air is breathtakingly hot and humid, even in the half-light of the under-forest, and thousands of tiny insects dance and twirl above the rotting vegetation of the forest floor.

A boy is moving silently among the trees, his younger sister walking behind him and complaining that she is tired. And hungry. And thirsty. The boy hushes her and tells her to wait – he knows a fruit that has sweet and thirst-quenching flesh. He gives the fruit a name, but his language has been lost. We would call it the language of the Olmec, but there are no written records of it.

The little sister begins to whine. Her brother shakes his head in irritation, and then suddenly stops. He can see the tree, he tells her. He can see the fruit.

His sister looks at the tree he is pointing to. It doesn't look particularly grand or special; it isn't very tall, the trunk is slender and blotched with lichen, and the branches are spindly.

All the same, she decides, it is quite a pretty tree: the top leaves are pink fading to a soft yellow, and the lower leaves are broad and a glossy green. Tiny clusters of pinky-white flowers grow directly from the trunk, as do a strange collection of differently sized fruits: some ridged, some smooth; some rough and some warty – as though the tree is experimenting with all kinds of sizes and shapes. The colours of the fruits vary too: pistachio green, pale yellow, orange deepening to crimson purple. The boy pauses and chooses a large oval fruit. He picks up a heavy stone with a sharp edge to hack it away from the tree, then uses the stone to break it open. It takes him several attempts; the rind is tough and thick. He hands half of the fruit to his sister, who has stopped grizzling and is looking on with interest.

"Suck the pulp, but spit out the seeds!" the boy instructs her, and she does as she is told. It tastes delicious, and takes away her thirst in moments. Her brother scoops out a fingerful of the sticky white pulp for himself, and takes pleasure in spitting the seeds as far away as he can. His sister begins to do the same, but then stops to inspect one. It's pale and almond-shaped, and when she bites it, it tastes bitter. She makes a face and spits.

"Told you," her brother says.

The little sister goes on sucking at the semi-translucent pulp, but she saves a handful of the seeds to play with later. She asks her brother for another fruit to take home, and he sighs but picks up his stone.

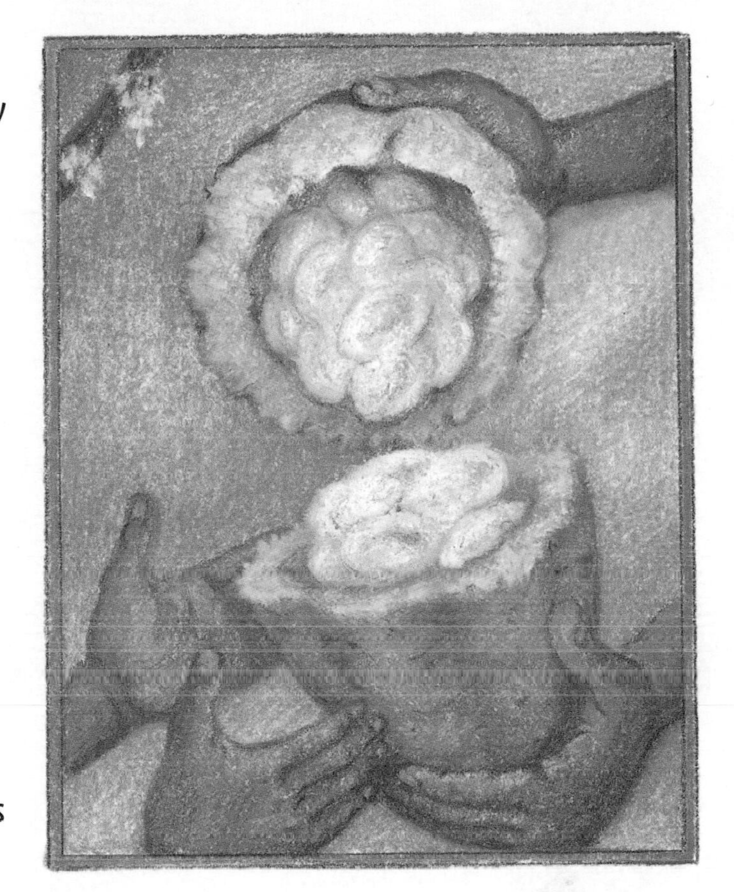

Later that day the fruit is split open. But the children have no chance to eat it. The little sister has scooped the contents into a rough wooden bowl and is just about to pick out the seeds, when her father arrives, panting. There's a feast in the neighbouring village; everyone is invited. The family hurry away and the seeds are left lying in the soft sweet pulp.

The feast lasts three days. By the time the family come back the pulp has melted into a vinegary liquid, and much of it has drained away through a crack in the old wooden bowl. The thirty or so seeds look darker. The mother is about to throw them away, but the little girl begs for them to play with, and spends the rest of the day arranging them in patterns on a bare slab

of rock. Her mother smiles and lets her play. The seeds stay drying on the rock for five days, and from time to time the girl arranges them into different patterns, or runs them between her fingers, turning them over and over. By the end of the five days the seeds have shrivelled a little and are hard and dry. The girl plays with them for a few more days, but eventually grows bored. She leaves them in a heap until later in the week when she sees her mother roasting meat. She wants to help; she wants to cook too! Her mother laughs at her, but the little girl insists ... and suddenly an idea occurs to her. Her seeds! She runs to fetch them, then tosses them onto the hot stone. As they heat, the outer shell cracks open and a curious smell fills the air.

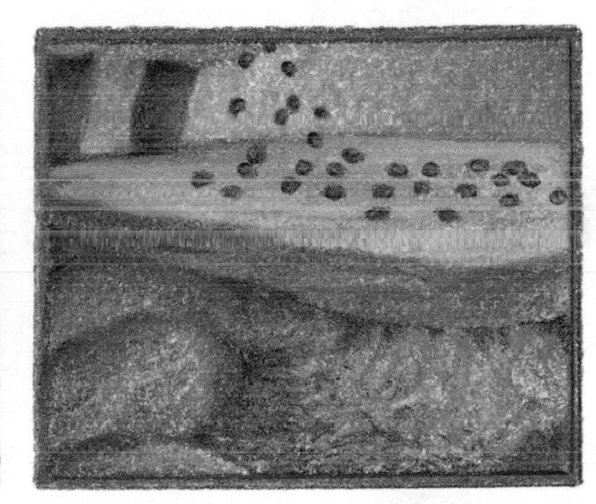

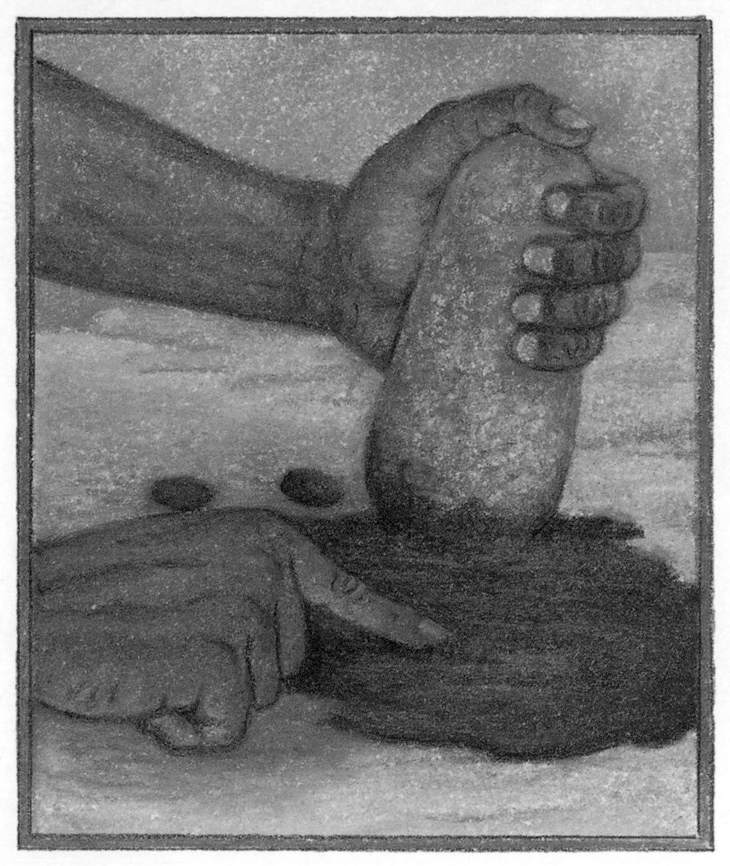

The little girl makes a face. She doesn't like the smell, and she loses interest and wanders off to play with her brother. Her mother, however, is intrigued. She has known this fruit all her life, but has never thought the seeds might be of any use. Eaten raw they are bitter and dry, and curl the tongue. No one in her tribe has ever thought of cooking them. She waits until they have cooled, shakes away the outer shells and looks curiously at the dark inner meat. She is used to grinding corn; she fetches her grinding stone and grinds the beans into a paste. Surprisingly, the paste glistens with an oily shine. She puts out a finger and tastes. She calls another woman and she tastes too. Other men and women

come to look; they taste,
and exclaim. They
experiment. More beans
are dried and roasted,
then ground into paste.
They mix the paste
with water, with spices,
with honey ... and
decide that the drink
they have invented is
a Very Excellent Thing.

Is that true? Who knows? And what happened once chocolate had been discovered? Different historians interpret the evidence in different ways, and a lot of so-called historical facts should be taken with a large pinch of salt (or a chunk of chocolate), especially when we're talking about 400 BCE. But this is what most people think happened.

THE BEAN AND THE OLMEC

The Olmec (that's only the name given to them by archaeologists and anthropologists – we have no idea what name they called themselves) lived in the rainforests alongside the cocoa or chocolate trees; we know that for certain. Did they discover the process of making the drink? Possibly. Unfortunately the tropical heat and heavy rain that are perfect for growing chocolate trees also rot away anything other than cold hard stone. All that is left of the Olmec are huge ceremonial pyramids and mounds, and massive stone heads. Maybe one day someone will unearth a monument with Olmec hieroglyphs describing the discovery of chocolate, but until then your guess is just as good as mine.

The Olmec civilization faded away, or collapsed, round about 400 BCE (it's impossible to tell quite why) and the areas where the Olmec lived were gradually taken over by the Maya people. It seems reasonable to assume there was a certain amount of overlap, so as the Maya moved into the areas where the cocoa trees grew, they would have learned about the making of chocolate from the former inhabitants. They went on to develop the process and to grow the trees in plantations.

North America
Yucatán Peninsula
South America

THE BEAN AND THE MAYA

The Maya civilization was highly sophisticated; the people built many beautiful cities, and distinctive pyramid-shaped temples. They also spent a great deal of time fighting each other; and when rival kings and princes were captured they were sacrificed with much splendour and ceremony. And what did they drink at these celebrations? Chocolate. We know this because the rich and important members of Maya society were buried in magnificent tombs together with beautifully carved and painted bowls, dishes and pots (so they had something to eat and drink in the afterlife, or on the way there).

The paintings included hieroglyphic writing in which the drinking of chocolate is regularly featured. In one of four Maya books that have survived there are pictures of various gods holding cocoa pods, with heaped dishes of pods close by. A vase has also been found decorated with a picture of a cocoa god. Cocoa pods are growing out of his arms and legs, and he's pointing at a chocolate pot in a meaningful kind of way.

But don't imagine the Maya settling down with steaming bowls of comforting hot chocolate. It was often a thick, gritty, bitter, COLD drink. There were all kinds of different flavours, and it was sometimes more of a porridge or a powder than a drink.

If the drink was made properly, the way the rich inhabitants of the palaces liked it, there was a thick froth on the top. The servants made this foam by pouring the chocolate from one container into another – usually from a high one into a much lower one. The froth was considered the best part of the drink, and with all those magical little bubbles bursting on your top lip it must have been the champagne of its time. There's nothing like bubbles to make a party go well!

The Maya survived up and into the ninth century CE. Then crop failures and endless wars caused the collapse of nearly all their city states. No civilization disappears completely; there are still pockets of Maya people alive today. And in the world of chocolate we owe the Maya a massive debt of gratitude. They were responsible for the word "cacao" and for turning the drinking of chocolate into an art form. They even used cocoa beans as small change. (Want a rabbit? That'll be ten beans, please.)

As the Maya civilization faded, a group of people known as the Toltecs moved in and took over the Yucatán peninsula. They remained in power for two centuries, then everything fell apart again – quite possibly because there was so much internal warring and fighting over the lands that produced the amazing cocoa crop. So, by the eleventh century, there was no strong and united opposition to prevent the powerful Aztec armies from reaching out and conquering their warring neighbours.

THE BEAN AND THE AZTECS

By the end of the fifteenth century the Aztecs had become the overlords of the main chocolate-growing areas on the coastal plains along the Pacific. They were highly sophisticated people, not at all the bloodthirsty savages some historians describe. There were priests, warriors and merchants, and the nobility enjoyed art and poetry, music and feasting. Many people were seriously rich – in our terms, there would have been hundreds of millionaires. And nearly all of this wealth came from trade, and from making areas they had conquered pay "tribute" – a kind of forced payment – much of which came in the form of cocoa beans.

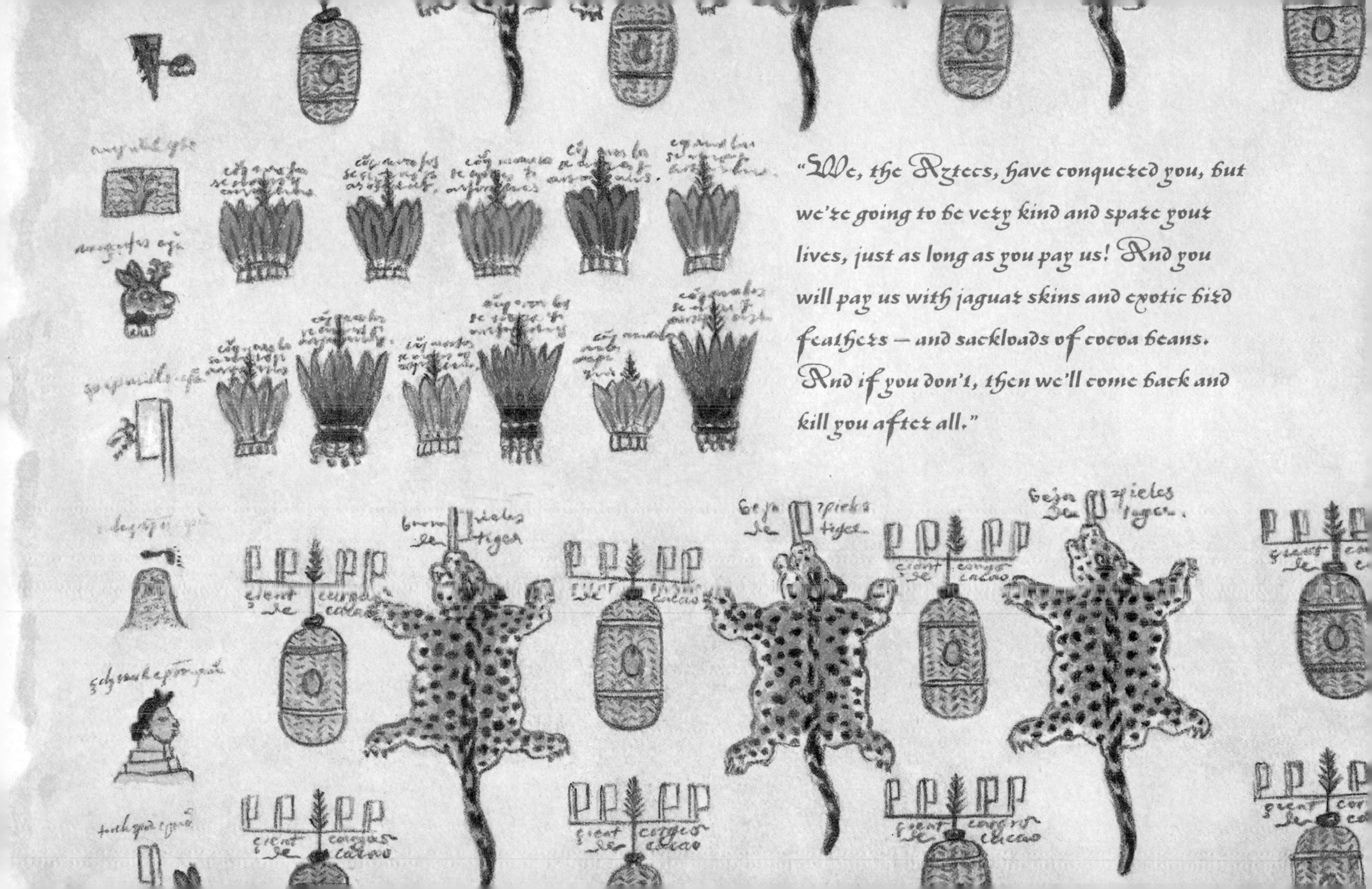

"We, the Aztecs, have conquered you, but we're going to be very kind and spare your lives, just as long as you pay us! And you will pay us with jaguar skins and exotic bird feathers – and sackloads of cocoa beans. And if you don't, then we'll come back and kill you after all."

Although drinking chocolate was a very important part of Aztec life, cocoa trees couldn't be grown in or near Tenochtitlan (the centre of Aztec civilization; today Mexico City) because the conditions were all wrong. The main source of the best-quality beans, Soconusco, was about 300 miles away, but some came from as far away as 500 miles. As there were no horses or carts, there must have been permanent trails of porters carrying sacks of beans along the tracks and roads. An average load was around 24,000 beans – pretty heavy!

We know some dealers tried to increase their profits by making fake beans out of clay. There are also records of sales of poor quality beans being treated to look like first-class. All tribute had to be counted because the Aztecs had not discovered the idea of weighing things. Just imagine having to count the 950 million cocoa beans in the emperor's warehouse bean by bean!

So why *did* the Aztecs think chocolate was so wonderful? Well, they were an odd bunch. In some ways they were very puritanical: they thought getting drunk was a complete abomination; it was punishable by death. There were two main drinks in the Aztec Empire, "octli" (alcoholic) and chocolate (non-alcoholic), so obviously chocolate was encouraged. Also, because it had to be imported, it was expensive and therefore had rarity value, and the rituals that surrounded the making and drinking of it were an added attraction. (There were thousands of recipes for different variations: hot, cold, honey-flavoured, chilli-flavoured, red, dark...)

Most importantly, chocolate was a drink for society's elite: royalty, nobles and high-ranking merchants. We know this because various drinking vessels have been found (some with chocolate grounds still at the bottom!), and these are made and decorated with such care that they were obviously bought and used by the rich. No rough clay pots or cups, the sort that would be used by everyday working people, have been discovered.

The Aztecs also believed that there was a spiritual quality in cocoa; they made a connection between chocolate and blood, possibly because a cocoa bean is more or less the same shape as a human heart. The heart contains blood; the bean contains chocolate – and both were thought essential for life and strength. Chocolate was part of the food ration given to every soldier on active service: ground cocoa was made into pellets and dried, and the soldiers would have added maize flour, water and probably some spices before drinking. It was also served at initiation ceremonies for high-ranking warriors who had completed all kinds of tests and reached the status of knight. It was a special reward for their bravery and "strong-heartedness".

Spanish missionaries who arrived in the sixteenth century learned the Aztec language so they could talk to the people and ask them how they had lived before strangers reached their shores. The written records they produced provide a great deal of information that would otherwise have been lost for ever, including an actual recipe for making Kukuh or Xocolat.

AN AZTEC RECIPE

Kukuh or Xocolat

INGREDIENTS

cocoa beans
a little cold water
chilli water
(Chop up red chillies, pour on boiling water and leave overnight. Then strain.)
vanilla pods
honey
pepper

1. Roast the cocoa beans in an open pan. When about three quarters of them have popped or split take them off the heat (if you leave them any longer they'll burn and taste horrid). Peel them as soon as they're cool enough to be handled.

2. With a pestle and mortar grind the peeled beans (the nibs) into a thick paste. Then put the paste into a clean, fine cloth and squeeze out as much of the oil as you can. Turn the paste out onto a tray and mould into little pellets. Leave overnight to dry.

3. Take enough pellets to fill one fifth of a cup/jug. Grind them back into paste with a little cold water and add chilli water, vanilla pods and a little honey. Pepper can be added to taste.

4. Boil up the mixture. As soon as it bubbles, take it off the heat. Allow to cool for five minutes then bring to the boil again. Do this at least five times, then allow to cool again. Just before drinking, hold the jug as high as you can reach and pour the mixture into a bowl on a lower surface. Do this several times until you have a thick foam, then drink

This recipe would have been known to most Aztecs, and they would have adjusted the amounts of chilli, pepper, vanilla and honey to suit their taste.

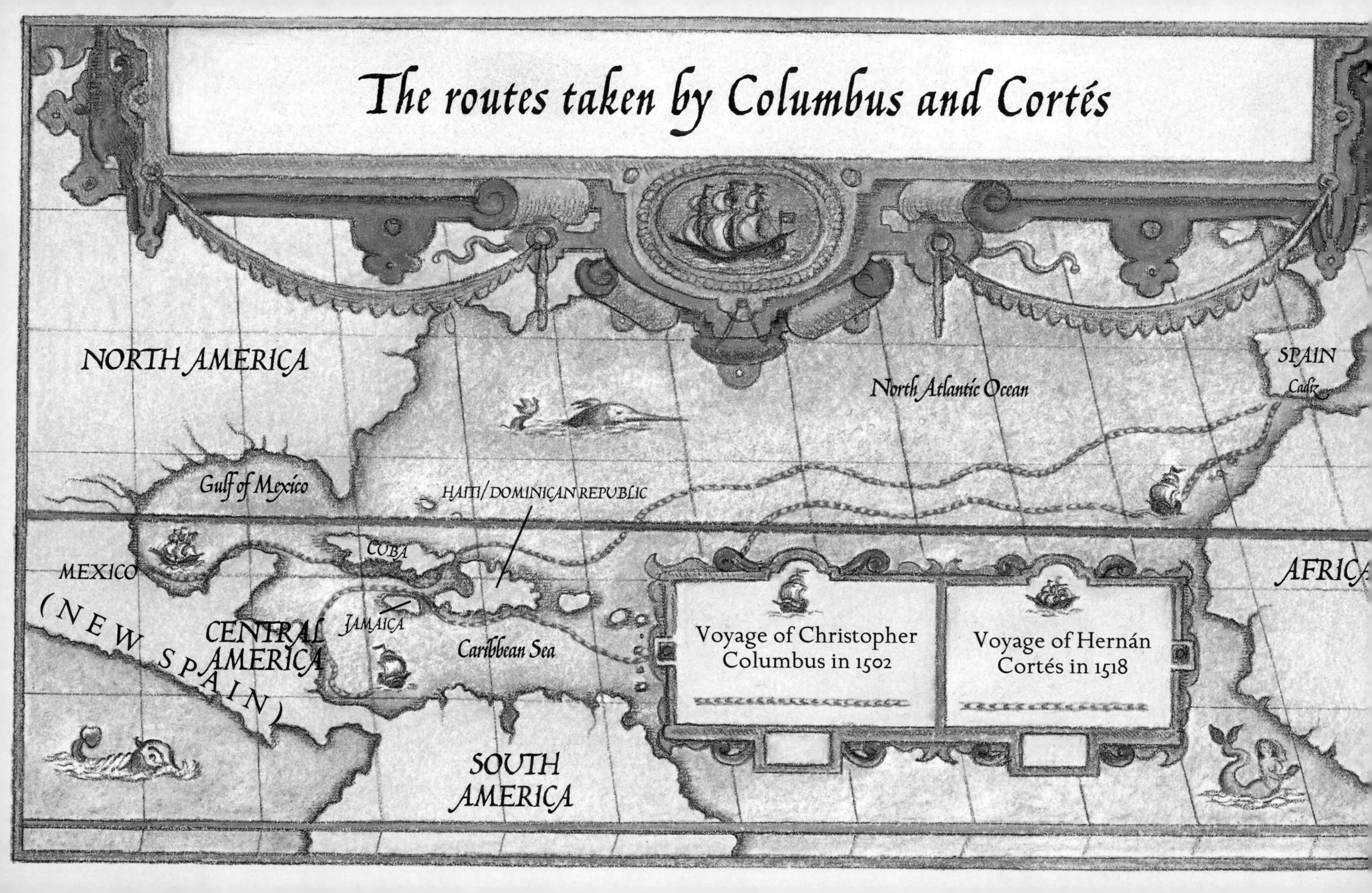

The routes taken by Columbus and Cortés
NORTH AMERICA
North Atlantic Ocean
SPAIN
Cadiz
Gulf of Mexico
HAITI/DOMINICAN REPUBLIC
CUBA
MEXICO
(NEW SPAIN)
JAMAICA
CENTRAL AMERICA
Caribbean Sea
AFRICA
Voyage of Christopher Columbus in 1502
Voyage of Hernán Cortés in 1518
SOUTH AMERICA

THE BEAN MEETS THE SPANISH

The Aztecs might well have continued in their way of life for many more centuries, and the drinking of chocolate gone unrecognized by the rest of the world; but the rest of the world was restless, and European explorers and traders were setting out to expand their lands and fortunes.

So along came the sixteenth century and something extraordinary happened in the story of the bean. From halfway across the world, a group of Spanish adventurers arrived in Mexico – and the Aztec Empire was destroyed.

The Spanish came because they were hunting for gold. The Aztecs were baffled by this – in their view cocoa beans were far more precious. But, to the Spanish, gold was fame, glory and, of course, wealth.

Christopher Columbus was the first to set foot in what came to be called New Spain. He put in a brief appearance in 1502, and his brother, Ferdinand, wrote in his diary that he had seen something that looked like almonds or *"some kind of bean that was much treasured by the Indians"*. However, seeing no signs of gold, Columbus sailed further south, and never explored the lands of the Aztecs.

The next arrival, Hernán Cortés, came in 1518 with a small army of soldiers. Gold was Cortés's obsession, along with a burning desire for lands and power. A ruthless man who had no time for anything that got in the way of what he wanted, he destroyed the Aztec Empire – some ten million people strong – with an army of 500 men and a great deal of cunning. And the Spanish discovered chocolate.

It took a while for the incoming settlers to appreciate the taste of cocoa. To begin with they saw how the beans were used as currency and were attracted to them for that reason only. It was an easy way to pay people; even better, you could swap handfuls of beans for gold. (Or slaves – 100 beans bought you a healthy male slave.)

Cortés took possession almost immediately of a large plantation of what he called "money trees". But when he and the other settlers saw how important drinking chocolate was to the Aztecs, they began to try it for themselves – and not just out of idle curiosity. In the sixteenth century the Spanish ate a very unhealthy diet (lots and lots of meat and fried food), so they had all kinds of health problems. Seeing the strong, healthy Aztecs must have made them hope that chocolate was a magic medicine found only in this new, strange land.

Some of the Spanish were hesitant to try the new drink because it was often mixed with something called "achiote", which stained your mouth a gory blood colour. But not everybody was put off. One of the best-known chocolate quotes, from a soldier, Girolamo Benzoni, is a brilliant example of the way people can change their minds!

"This drink seems more like pig swill than a drink for men. I was in this country more than a year, and never wished to taste of it, and when I passed by dwellings some Indian would offer me a drink, and when I refused would go away with much laughter.

But given that I did not have a store of wine and could not always drink water, I decided to do as the others. This drink is in flavour somewhat bitter, it satisfies and refreshes the body, and does not cause drunkenness, and is the most expensive and important merchandise of that country."

Once families began to arrive, it was natural for the exchange of traditional foods and styles of cooking to take place. ("You try my recipe and I'll try yours!") Ships came from Spain bringing sacks of wheat, sheep, pigs and cows (the Spanish were horrified to discover that there was no cheese in Mexico), and local foods were tried and tested as well. An important import from Europe was sugar. The incomers soon realized that this new world was ideal for growing sugar cane. Given that just about everything tasted better with sugar added, why not mix some with this new drink?

Result: *Deee*-licicious! (Well, after a few trials and experiments.)

It wasn't long before the Spaniards thought of chocolate as the new must-have delicacy. It was good for you in all kinds of ways, they decided – a positive tonic that cured you when you felt faint and strengthened your body against disease. Records show that fine ladies even drank it in church, a practice which was eventually banned.

I imagined a young boy's diary from the time...

The Feast of Saint Boniface, June 5th

Today my mama took us, as always on a saint's day, to High Mass at San Cristobal. There was such a chill in the cathedral as to make our flesh shiver. The High Mass began with much ceremony and droning of Latin, and it was but a short time before my little sister began to pluck at our mother's sleeve. My mother was also restless, and instead of reproving my sister and bidding her attend the sacred words, she bent her finger to one of our maids who stood behind. At once the maid left the building, only to return before many minutes had passed with a fine, tall jug of that much-loved delicacy, chocolate. I perceived clearly that the priest was not pleased with this proceeding, and he was frowning mightily; but there was little that he could do. By the time of his sermon the click-clack of the wooden shoes of many maids coming to and fro with cups of sweet-smelling chocolate all but drowned his words.

July 20th

It is now several weeks since my last diary entry. My mother is much angered. The bishop of San Cristobal has forbidden the presence of gluttonous substances in that holy place, naming the drinking of excessive quantities of chocolate as a sin. The very last time she attended the cathedral, priests were standing at the door, and, as the maids click-clacked in with their mistresses' refreshment, they attempted to seize it from them! Much was spilled, and finely dressed ladies were heard screaming, my mother among the loudest and most forceful of complainants.

My father sighs, and rides more often instead of attending Mass. I go with him.

August 7th

My mother is once more content, and my sister also. They now attend the Convent of Saint Mary and All the Angels, where the taking of chocolate is accepted by all. She says that the holy nuns have a gift for making it that is "nothing less than divine".

THE BEAN LEAVES HOME

How did the bean begin to travel?

Quick answer: no one knows. But it reached Spain and settled there for some time before it travelled on.

Various historians have said Cortés was the first importer of chocolate to Europe, but there aren't any records proving this. There's a long list of things he did bring back in 1528 (including one of the Aztec emperor Moctezuma's sons and bouncing rubber balls), but chocolate and cocoa beans aren't mentioned. What we do know is that, in 1544, a party of missionary priests sailed back to Spain with a group of Maya nobles, bringing gifts of feathers, spices and chocolate for Prince Philip of Spain, though there's nothing to say whether the prince said "yuck!" or "yippeee!"

The first properly recorded shipment of cocoa beans from New Spain to Seville was in 1585, but that doesn't mean that chocolate wasn't known about before then. The chances are that it was, because it quickly became very popular in Spanish monasteries and convents.

Just as in its country of origin, chocolate was a luxury item in Spain. This was mainly because it was very expensive (think how far it had to travel), and fashionable courtiers liked to think of it as an exclusive kind of medicinal drink. In its simplest form it was made from cocoa pastilles or tablets, sugar, cinnamon and vanilla; but very often other ingredients were added, such as chillies or pepper, sometimes even rose flavouring!

The Spanish also ATE chocolate; solid chocolate sweets were a particular delicacy at elegant banquets, although they were known to taste gritty, make your fingers very messy – and they fell apart almost

as soon as you touched them unless they were made with honey, which made them hideously sticky.

When you were ready for your drinking chocolate, your maid would break up the correct amount of dried pastille and put it into a special jug that had a lid with a hole in it. Hot water was added, and a kind of swizzle stick (called a *molinillo*) was inserted through the hole and used to whizz the mixture round and round until it was thick and frothy.

Once the shipping of cocoa beans had begun, there was no stopping it. Ships sailed out with supplies for the colonists and came back laden with new and exciting cargoes.

People got very rich but it was a dangerous business. I imagined two letters, one from a Spanish merchant who was very excited about making money from cocoa beans, the other from an English pirate who robbed him, but didn't know what the beans were...

May 1588

My darling Caterina,

Our fortune will soon be made! I met with a sea captain in this port whose ship the *Santa Felicia* is bound for Guatemala, on the coast of the New Spain. He is due there with a cargo of wheat for those brave souls who have begun new lives far away across the sea. I have given this captain orders to bring me back a cargo of cocoa beans, which I shall sell at a high profit. Then I shall buy you a little horse for your very own, and as many other playthings as your heart desires.

I must wait here to see this ship come safely home and to arrange for the sale of her most wonderful cargo. I must also repay certain moneys that I have had to borrow, but we shall be the happiest family in Castile when all is done.

I remain your very loving

Papa

June 1589

To Mam, my love, and a kiss to sister Sal. We made good speed from Engeland to the place they call New Spain. Our shippe is arrow fast. We have not seen whales, but many fish that fly high. I was not sikke in the storms, but two men were washed by mighty waves into the deep and gone for ever, may their souls be with God. Still we seek our fortune. Yesterday our captain was high of hope as we saw a fat Spanish shippe, the *Santa Felícia,* lying low near the shore. But when we grappled and boarded there was naught in the hold but sacks of sheep's droppings, though smelling strange indeed. The captain ordered one sack opened for thinking that gold might be hidden, but there was none. In anger he ordered the shippe to be put to fire. The flames roared high and black smoke hung low for long after we had set sail once more. No sheep's droppings ever smelled like that in Engeland.

Your loving son,

Judd

THE BEAN HAS PROBLEMS

By the end of the sixteenth century the Spanish were firmly established in New Spain – but all was not well. In the 80 years or so they had been there, they had wiped out an extraordinary 90 per cent of the native population. And not only through warfare, punishment and ill-treatment – the European invaders had brought European diseases with them. The native inhabitants had no resistance to smallpox, measles, influenza, and other illnesses besides, and they died in huge numbers.

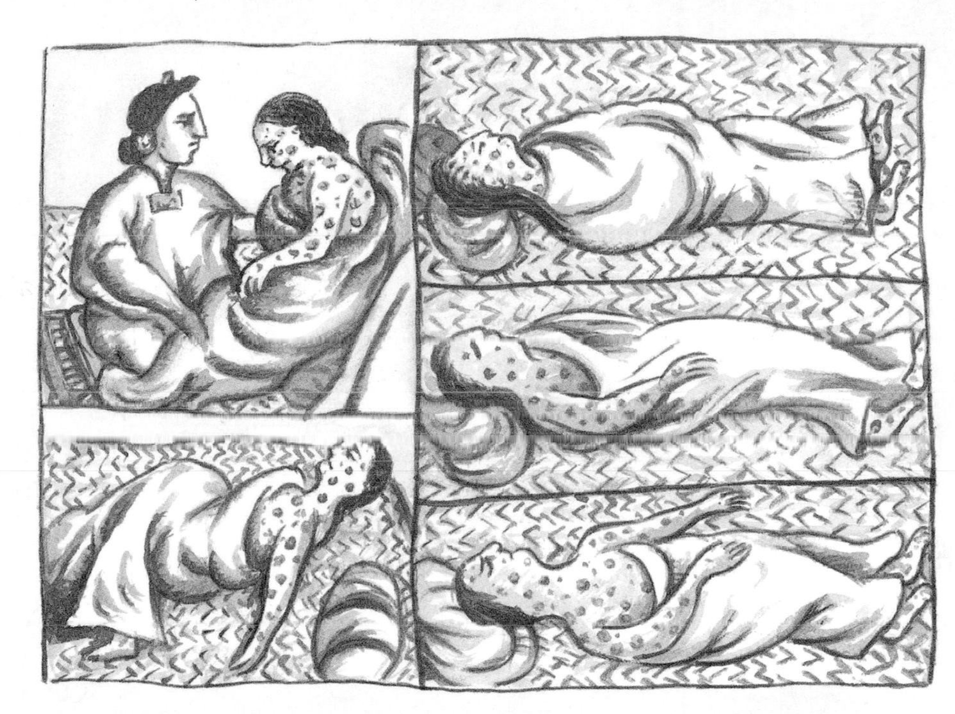

Gradually this became a big problem for the colonists. The Spanish government had given Spanish families who wanted to move to South America a piece of land, together with the people living on it, who were expected to provide free labour. But these free labourers (slaves under a different name) were dying. Soon not enough people knew how to grow and harvest the chocolate trees, and crops began to fail.

This meant that, by the beginning of the seventeenth century, the Spanish had to look elsewhere for suitable areas to grow their much sought-after beans. Ecuador, Venezuela and Trinidad had the right climate, as did Jamaica.

As plantations spread around the world there was obviously a need for cheap labour to look after them, and by the time people realised how much money could be made from chocolate, the slave trade was in existence. There is a lot written about how slaves were seized in West Africa and brought to the colonies to work on sugar plantations; but there were as many people living appalling and miserable lives on the estates where cocoa beans were grown. Chocolate and

sugar: neither were (or are!) essential food stuffs; but they were lusted after by the rich and produced by men and women who lived lives of indescribable poverty and deprivation.

While people were suffering to grow and harvest the bean in one part of the world, in another part of the world chocolate was becoming hugely popular among people who knew little or nothing about how it was produced.

SIGNOR BEAN

From Spain, chocolate began to travel across Europe. It was certainly known in Italy in the 1640s, when it was mentioned in a medical pamphlet, and, in 1686, the scholar Giuseppe Donzelli wrote that it was good for the digestion.

Most wealthy people in Europe in the seventeenth century had a bad diet. They ate meat cooked with a lot of fat and very few vegetables, and they drank alcohol at every meal. (Water was nearly always undrinkable, especially in towns and cities – because there were no sewers, the water supplies carried diseases.) They also adored cheese and

anything sweet – the more sugar became available, the more it was consumed. All of which added up to fairly constant bloating, agonizing wind, constipation, fierce indigestion and other stomach problems. This in turn resulted in an obsession with new medicinal foods or drinks that might make them feel better. Mostly, the poor were a great deal healthier than the rich – they ate many more vegetables, and were lucky if they had meat once a week.

In those days, people believed all food and drink had the ability to warm you up or cool you down, soothe you or make you strong – and chocolate was thought particularly good as a tonic or strengthening medicine. A famous Italian scientist and doctor, Francesco Redi, invented a special jasmine-flavoured chocolate for the ducal court of Tuscany, a recipe he kept strictly secret until his death in 1697. He added fresh jasmine flowers, sugar, vanilla beans, cinnamon and "two scruples of ambergris" to roasted, peeled and crushed cocoa beans. It was claimed that this particular recipe kept the ruler of Tuscany, Cosimo III, alive until he was 80 – which was not a good thing, as he was a most unpleasant man.

And there was another more creepy use for chocolate – as a disguise. The slightly bitter taste of the cocoa and spices covered up the taste of most poisons very well, and there are many cases of poisoning by chocolate on record. In 1774 Pope Clement XIV died under extremely suspicious circumstances (he'd been terrified of being assassinated for years) and it was believed that he had been poisoned by a dish of chocolate.

The confectioner who had provided the chocolate drank some as well, and he died too which seems pretty conclusive.

But the Spanish and Italian clergy believed passionately in chocolate as a medicine, and it may well have moved on to France when the Cardinal of Lyon fell ill. Apparently he was told by some Spanish monks that this amazing drink would cure him.

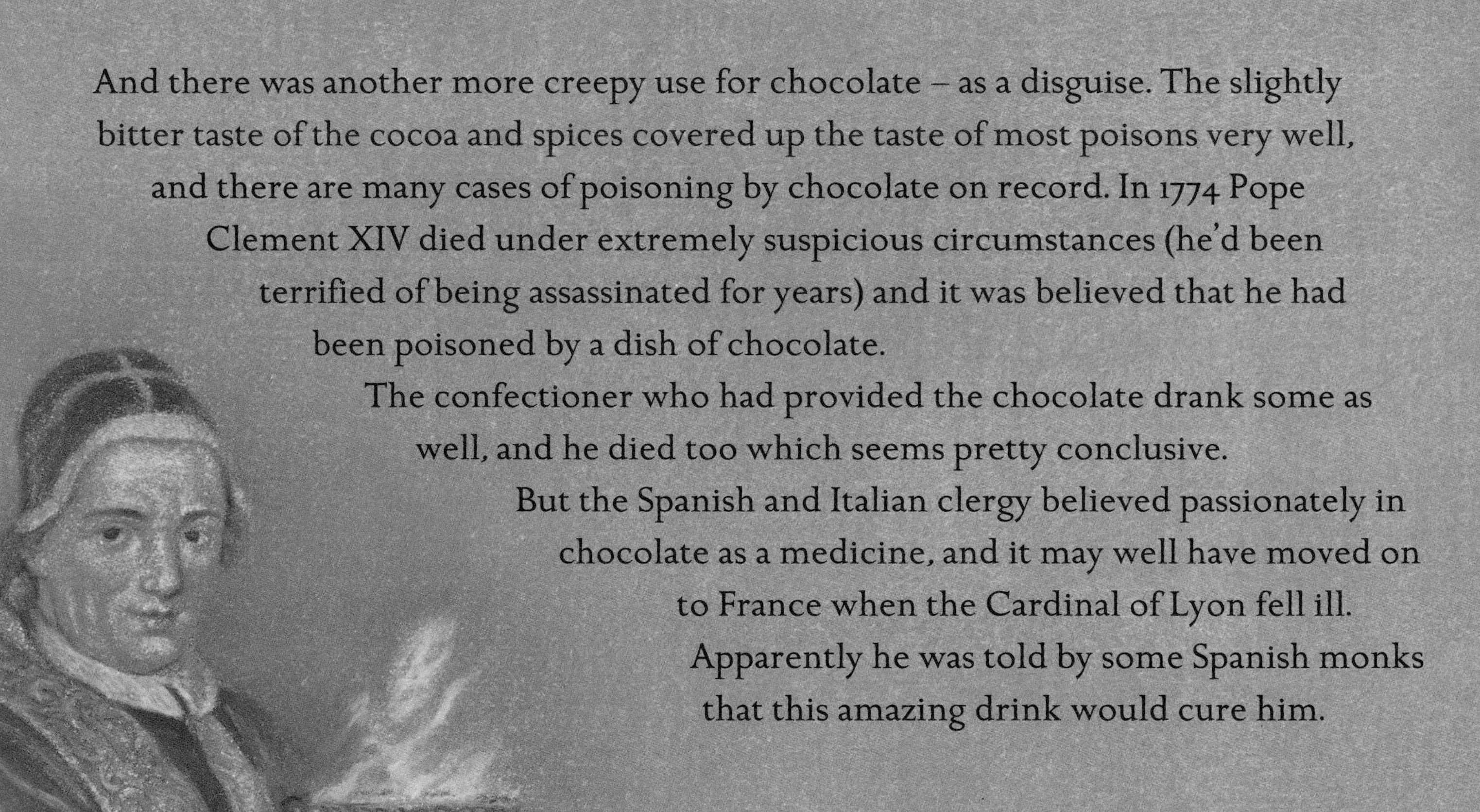

MONSIEUR BEAN

What is certain is that, in 1659, a man called Daniel Chaliou was given exclusive rights to make and sell chocolate throughout the kingdom of France. He could sell it in liquid form, in boxes or as tablets, and by 1670, drinking chocolate was a very fashionable and well-known habit. The French aristocracy took to it like ducks to water.

There's a description in *A Tale of Two Cities* by Charles Dickens of a Monseigneur being given his morning chocolate just before the revolution began in 1789.

> One lacquey carried the chocolate-pot into the sacred presence; a second, milled and frothed the chocolate with the little instrument he bore for that function; a third, presented the favoured napkin; a fourth poured the chocolate out...

The chocolate was still frothed up by a *molinillo,* which the French called a *moussoir.* The chocolate-pot or *chocolatière* was made of silver, unless the owner was sufficiently grand to own a gold one. It became an essential part of every fine lady and gentleman's household; if you wanted to give someone a particularly splendid present you would order them a wonderfully decorated *chocolatière* or a set of beautiful porcelain cups and saucers.

Most recipes for drinking chocolate still consisted of cocoa beans, sugar, vanilla and cinnamon; the use of chillies was gradually fading out, and a very good thing too, as far as I'm concerned. In the interests of proper research I tried a cup of chocolate made with chillies according to a seventeenth-century French recipe, and I can only say that it took me about twenty-seven glasses of water before I felt as if I might, just possibly, survive until the next day! My entire mouth and throat felt as if they were on fire. It was disgustingly thick and gritty, and there was a weird kind of oiliness about it. If you want to experiment (at your own risk!) here are the ingredients.

Chocolat

This is based on a recipe written down by a Monsieur St Disdier in France in 1692.

INGREDIENTS
900 g cocoa nibs
450 g fine sugar
9 g cinnamon
7 g chilli pepper
7 g cloves (powdered)
35 g vanilla

Grind the cocoa nibs (roasted beans separated from their husks and broken into little pieces) with the sugar and the spices. Then boil everything up in about 200 ml of water, simmer for ten minutes or longer, and finally froth up with a food mixer.

MR BEAN

And what was happening across the channel in England? If you remember, before 1600 English pirates thought cocoa beans were sheep's droppings. But not long after, a traveller to England reported that the aristocracy were drinking chocolate in large quantities "as both Diet and Physick". Samuel Pepys, the diary writer, was a great fan who regularly drank his "morning draught in good Chocolatte".

But there were also a number of disapproving comments suggesting that the English were abandoning the traditional ways of making chocolate and ruining the true flavour.

> "The chocolatte that was served me in the cittee of London was lacking flavor or spice of any kinde, and was spoild from exceeding much of sugar and burnt milk," wrote a despairing French visitor.

Special "houses of entertainment" called "Chocolate Houses" sprang up, where men with time on their hands could go and drink a cup of chocolate, smoke and discuss the events of the day. One of these, Francis White's Chocolate House in St James's, became a famous gentleman's club.

Chocolatte

This English recipe would have been recognized by chocolate drinkers round about 1700 (and now as well!).

INGREDIENTS
100g chocolate without sugar
100g sugar
a little salt
7 g flour or starch
1 litre of wholesome milk
(In the seventeenth and eighteenth centuries milk was usually sour, watered down and full of germs that might well kill you – or, at the very least, give you appalling food poisoning – so it was important to use fresh, healthy milk.)

Mix together until well dissolved, boil and serve.

THE BEAN GOES FURTHER

And it wasn't just the people of Spain, France, Italy and England who were turning into chocoholics in the seventeenth century. In Holland, the Dutch East India Company had become one of the leading importers of cocoa beans. Germany and Switzerland were also hugely enthusiastic. There were regional variations in the way chocolate was prepared – for example, rich Germans sometimes mixed it with wine before adding hot water – but right across Europe the tiny cocoa bean was growing in importance by the day.

So what of the new colonies in North America? And the rest of the world? The habit of drinking chocolate travelled surprisingly slowly to the dinner tables of families in Massachusetts and other colonies in North America. You might have thought that it would have made its way up from the South, but it's generally agreed that, to start with, it bounced back from across the Atlantic. There are records of cargoes of beans crossing the Atlantic from South America to Europe, and then crossing back again to North America in the early 1700s, but the most important date seems to be 1765, when John Hannon brought cocoa beans directly from the West Indies to Dorchester, Massachusetts. In that same year he and James Baker set up a business to process the beans themselves. The Americans took to chocolate with enthusiasm, but it didn't go down so well beyond Europe in the other direction – even today chocolate isn't enthused over in India or China. The Russians and the Australians love chocolate though, and there are a number of very successful chocolate factories in New Zealand.

THE BEAN HITS THE BIG TIME

As the years rolled on, chocolate-drinking continued to be enjoyed by those who could afford it. But changes were taking place in society that were going to alter dramatically the way the little bean was thought of. For centuries it had been the upper classes – the landowners – who had the money to buy good things like chocolate, and it had been accepted that the rich were rich and the poor were poor, and that was the way God had arranged things. But by the end of the seventeenth century some business people had become extremely rich and the cities buzzed with a new kind of person, "the self-made man". Suddenly you could rise from the humblest of backgrounds and become rich – and enjoy all the treats and delights you fancied. As businesses grew, so did the idea of making things on a larger and larger scale. Products were cheaper and more people could afford them, which led to MORE and BIGGER factories. This extraordinary time of massive manufacturing was called ... THE INDUSTRIAL REVOLUTION!

Thanks to new machines, the cocoa bean found itself being processed and turned into chocolate at a speed the Aztecs could never have dreamt of. Inventors worked night and day to develop new processes and keep ahead of their competitors.

It is true that the Aztecs had made chocolate into tablets or solid blocks, and it had been eaten in many different forms as a sweetmeat or delicacy for hundreds of years. (This habit increased once the chocolate was mixed with sugar before it was dried, because sugar made it far less bitter.) But it would be fair to say that solid chocolate, made for the specific purpose of being eaten, grew into a major industry at the end of the nineteenth century. It may seem very odd to us that this had never happened before but how would you feel if I said I had some amazing solid tea for you to eat? We don't connect tea in any way with something that can be nibbled at while watching our favourite TV programme, even though we've all seen tea leaves. From the first discovery of the cocoa tree, chocolate had been thought of as a drink, a special drink that was taken in company, often with an enormous amount of ritual and ceremony. It had travelled the

world with all kinds of claims for its magical powers and medicinal potency, and was an accepted part of civilized life. In some ways it's more extraordinary that it *did* become the huge money-making delicacy that we know (and love!) today. It had, after all, been a drink for at least 3000 years.

So – how did eating chocolate come about? Was it one person, one country, one amazing invention?

No, it was a cross-fertilization of discoveries and methods from many different places across Europe. As you will see...

IMPORTANT INVENTIONS

1795 Joseph Fry of Bristol bought a "Watts" steam engine to grind cocoa beans. This meant chocolate could be produced on a much larger scale, so the price came down. Joseph Fry was a Quaker and he felt strongly that the huge amount of alcohol drunk by the "working classes" of his day led to people losing their jobs or doing them unsatisfactorily – or not at all – as well as great unhappiness and eventual ruin. His hope was to produce a drink that was healthy, non-alcoholic and cheap enough to be bought by those on a very low income.

The first Cadbury was a Quaker as well, a bright young man called John. In 1824 he opened a tea and coffee shop in Birmingham and by 1831 he too had begun to manufacture cocoa and drinking chocolate. The Frys and the Cadburys continued as rivals for the rest of the century and beyond. You can still buy chocolate with the name Fry on it, but it's owned by Cadbury now – they bought his firm.

1828 The Dutchman Coenraad Van Houten invented a new hydraulic press that was much more efficient at squeezing the oil, or cocoa butter, from the cocoa beans. This was called Dutching, after its inventor.

This invention is a very important one in the story of chocolate. It meant that much more of the cocoa butter could be removed, and the "cake" that was left could easily be ground into a fine powder. Van Houten experimented and found that if he added alkalizing salts the powder mixed well with water, and the resulting chocolate drink, which we know as "cocoa", was milder and easier to digest. News of this invention zoomed round Europe, and dutching became an essential part of making chocolate from then on.

1847 Francis Fry – grandson of Joseph – mixed melted cocoa butter, sugar and cocoa powder together, instead of the usual cocoa powder, sugar and water. The mixture was poured into a mould and as it cooled, it set into a bar!

These bars, which were exhibited in 1849, were called *Chocolat Délicieux à Manger*, and were, as far as we are able to tell, the first proper chocolate bars. The bars and tablets that had been made before with pure chocolate and sugar were very fragile, and fell apart

much too easily. There was an enormous demand for this new treat; as a result the price of cocoa butter went up, and the price of cocoa powder went down. But the Fry family were not as well recognized for this new invention as they could have been: when Queen Victoria chose her royal supplier of chocolate in 1855, she chose the Cadburys! And after that the Cadbury family had one success after another.

In 1866 Cadbury's Cocoa Essence appeared on the market and in 1868 came the first chocolate box. It had a picture of Jessica Cadbury holding a kitten on the lid. Sales boomed.

1879 Rodolphe Lindt of Switzerland invented conching, a process which hugely improved the texture and quality of chocolate by heating and rolling it.

This got rid of the last of the grittiness that had been part of the chocolate experience ever since it was first discovered. The resulting smoothness allowed the chocolate to melt on the tongue ... mmmmm!

1879 Daniel Peter, a Swiss chocolate-maker, combined his chocolate with powdered milk made by Henri Nestlé – and made the first ever milk chocolate bar.

From then on there were lots of refinements and experiments in the balance of cocoa powder, butter and sugar, but, basically, eating chocolate as we know it had been invented. In 1893 an American, Milton Hershey, saw German chocolate-making machinery on show at an exhibition in Chicago, which he then imported all the way from Dresden. At first he used it to coat caramels in chocolate, but then, in 1894, he went on to make his first "candy bars" and a whole new chocolate empire was founded in America.

1908 Switzerland invented its own favourite chocolate bar, Toblerone.
Did you know those triangle shapes are meant to represent Alpine peaks?

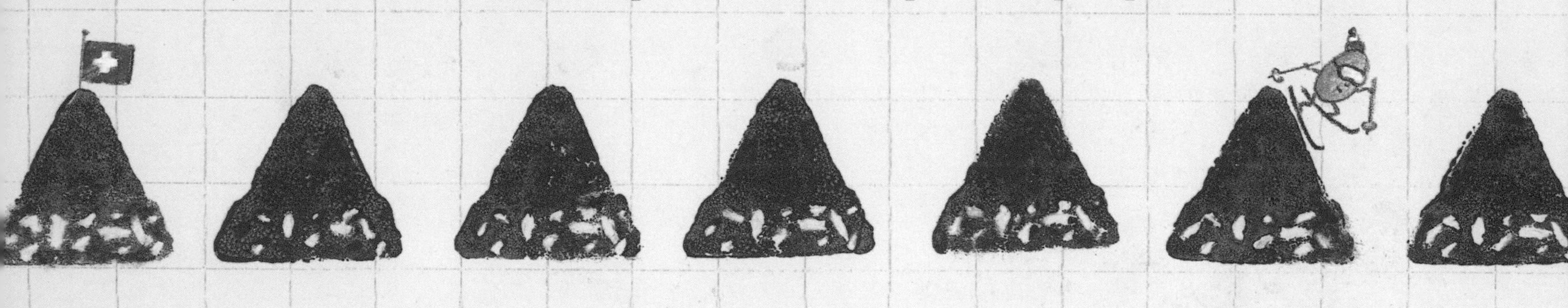

1933 Chocolate chip cookies arrive.
The story goes that Ruth Wakefield, an American cook, was making chocolate biscuits and threw in lumps of chocolate, expecting that they would melt during baking. They didn't – and the result was the famous chocolate chip cookie.

The inventions went on, and some of them were popular and some of them fell out of favour. But, overall, an enormous amount of money is still made out of chocolate: 73.2 billion dollars in 2001 – a 21 per cent increase from 1996 (42 per cent of this profit was made by European manufacturers).

CHOCOLATE TREES

1. Chocolate trees are technically called cocoa, or cacao, trees (pronounced cackow). The latin name is *Theobroma cacao*; *Theobroma* means something like "food of the gods".

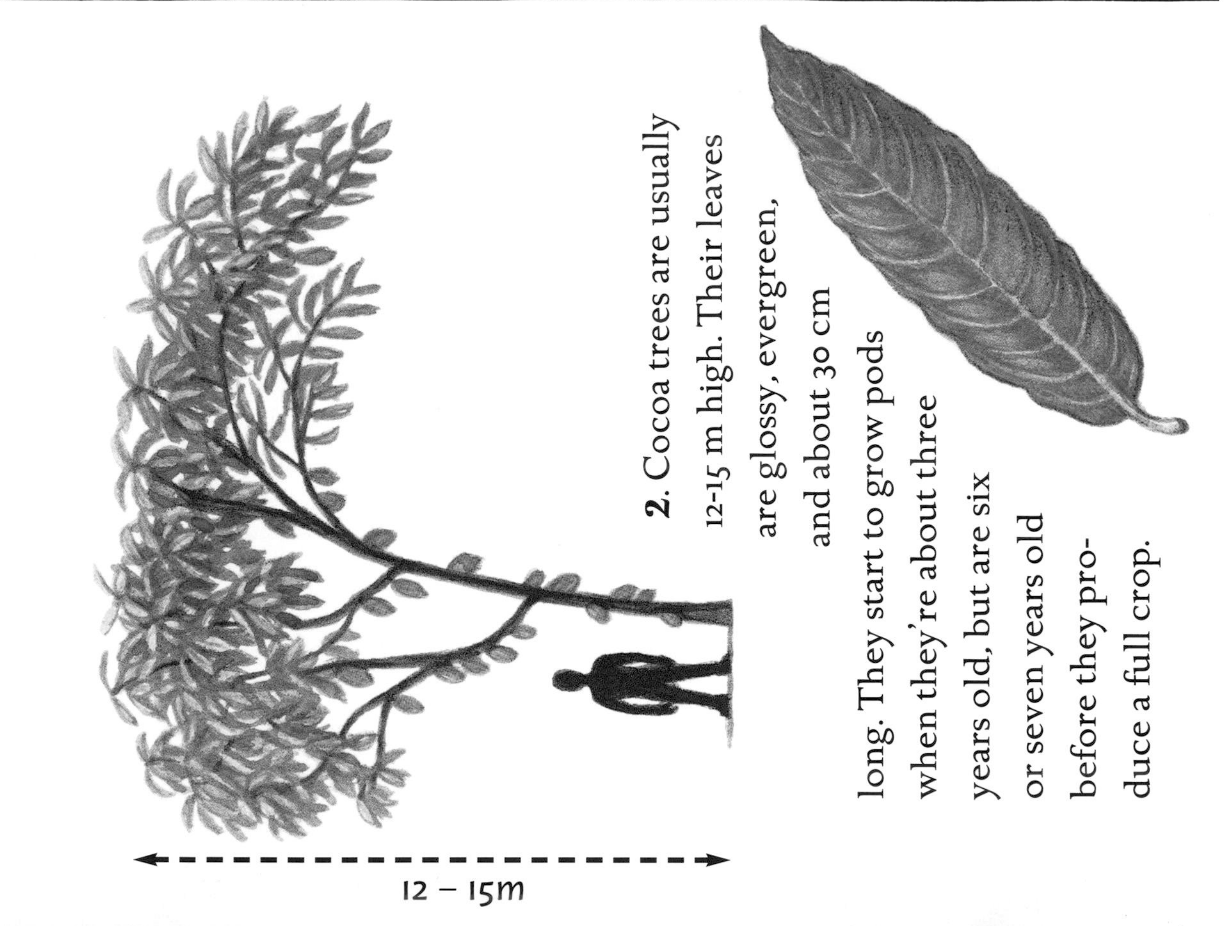

2. Cocoa trees are usually 12-15 m high. Their leaves are glossy, evergreen, and about 30 cm long. They start to grow pods when they're about three years old, but are six or seven years old before they produce a full crop.

3. The trees, which grow naturally in the rainforests, are more often found in big plantations these days, as the crop is so important. They need a high average temperature (more or less a steady 27 °C) and non-stop high humidity, preferably from regular rainfall (some growers try to recreate this humidity with permanent misting, but that is very expensive). The soil has to be well drained and full of nutrients. The earth in the rainforests is ideal as it is made up of deep-rotting vegetation, and growers have to try and recreate this natural compost. If the soil is too clean there's a serious problem: the tiny midges that pollinate the flowers disappear, so there's no pollination and no pods form.

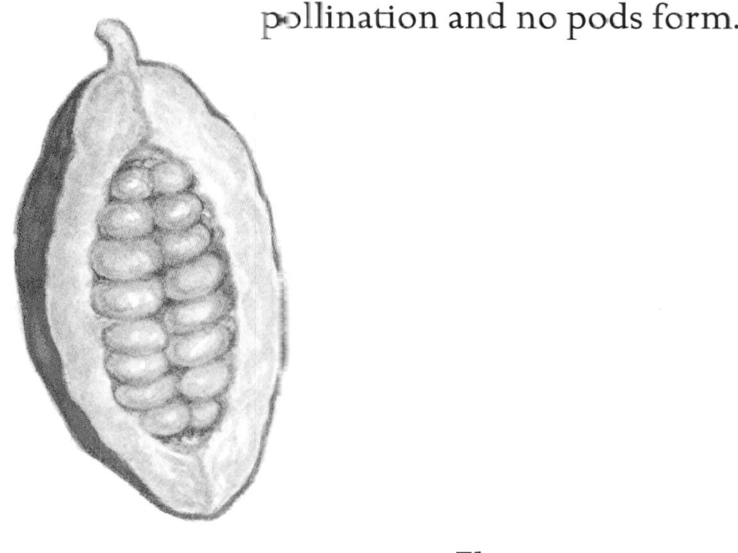

4. The flowers on the cocoa tree are very small and grow straight out of the trunk and branches. They grow all year round, and someone once counted the number of flowers on a single tree on one particular day and reckoned there were about a hundred thousand. They grow in little clusters, and after they have been pollinated, tiny green pods form. But that doesn't mean there are thousands of pods on each tree – different experts have different estimates, but most agree that only one to five per cent of the flowers produce fruit.

5. Many diseases and pests attack cocoa trees. Insects feed on the sap and damage the plant. There's a moth (the Cocoa Pod Borer Moth) that lays its eggs on the tree, then its larvae bore into the pods , so the beans don't develop properly. And if you really want to upset a cocoa farmer, just whisper the words "Black Pod Disease". This is a horrible fungus that whips through a plantation making the pods rot away. Then there's Frosty Pod Rot, and the wonderfully named Witches' Broom Disease – another fungus that attacks flowers and pods as well as new leaf buds. Witches' Broom wiped out nearly half of the cocoa trees in Brazil in the 1990s.

6. If a flower does develop into a pod, and the pod stays healthy, it'll take about six months to grow to a size that's ready to harvest. Some pods weigh as much as a kilo, while others are much smaller; it depends on the type of tree. There isn't a regular time to harvest them; a grower usually comes round every two to four weeks to collect the ripe fruit. The most successful growers know exactly when a pod is ripe for picking, and it's not easy – they don't have any particular shape or colour that says Pick Me Now! (In fact, there can be lots of different coloured pods on the same tree ... very confusing if you're not an expert.)

Hopefully there will be between thirty and forty-five beans in each pod.

7. If you want to grow a cocoa tree for yourself, go and live somewhere between 20 ° north and 20 ° south of the equator. Preferably in a rainforest. And don't plant your tree too high, because winds can damage the crop.

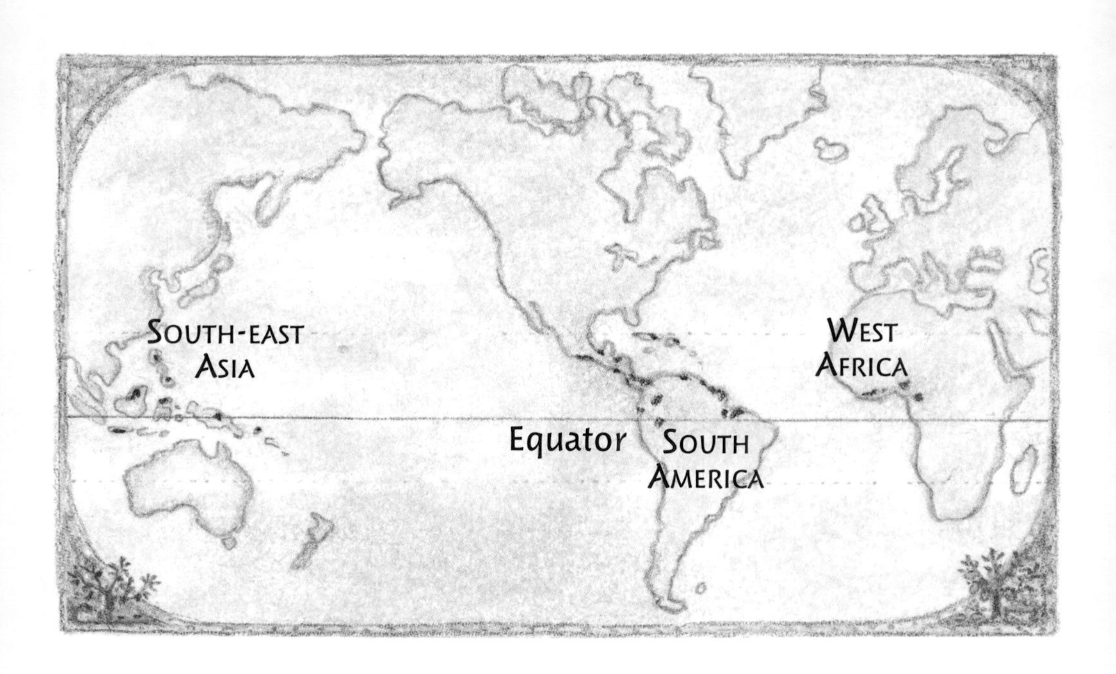

8. The three major cocoa-growing regions of the world are South America, West Africa and South-east Asia. In 2003, 34,000 tonnes of cocoa beans were harvested worldwide.

9. There are two distinct varieties of cocoa – or cacao – tree; one is called Criollo and produces the very best-quality chocolate. Criollo trees are very fragile, though – if there are any diseases going round they'll catch them. The other is called Forastero; the chocolate isn't so good, but the trees are much tougher. There's also a type of tree called Trinitario, which is the result of cross-pollination, so it's half Criollo and half Forastero. It appeared in the eighteenth century in Trinidad, after the Criollo trees were almost completely wiped out. Forastero seedlings were brought in, and the two, as it were, got together. You'd think Trinitario trees would be the ideal solution because they're tougher than the Criollo but have a better-quality chocolate than the Forastero. But chocolate experts say that absolutely nothing beats a true Criollo chocolate.

HOW CHOCOLATE IS MADE

1. HARVESTING. The pods are cut off the tree using machetes or sharp knives on sticks. (So far no one has managed to invent a machine that can pick cocoa beans.)

2. The pods are opened and the beans pulled out. They are covered in a white pulp, which is mostly taken off by hand – a very squelchy operation.

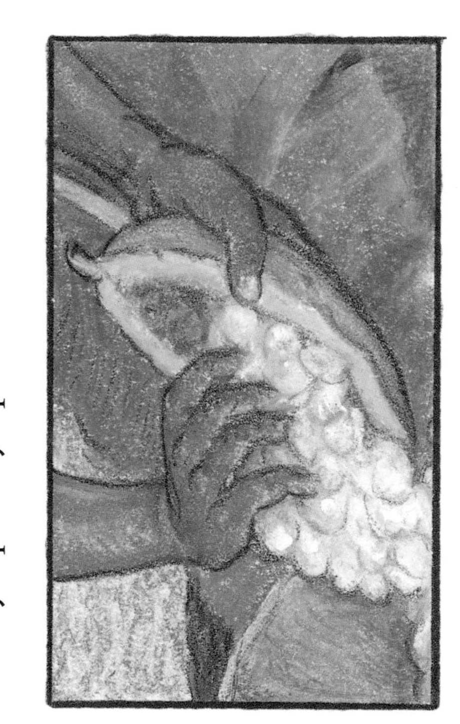

3. FERMENTATION. This is something that happens to any fruit or vegetable if you leave it for a few days – it's really the first stage of it going rotten. The bean gets very hot as it lies in the sun and this kills it so it can't grow. Its chemical make-up changes as well, which completely alters the flavour. (The fresh bean doesn't taste of chocolate at all. You'd never guess how it was going to end up!)

There are two sorts of fermentation: HEAP and BOX. In heap fermentation (mostly used in West Africa) up to 2500 kg of beans are heaped up with what remains of the white sticky pulp, covered with banana leaves, and left for five to six days. Sometimes the farmers turn the beans over halfway through, especially if the heap is large.

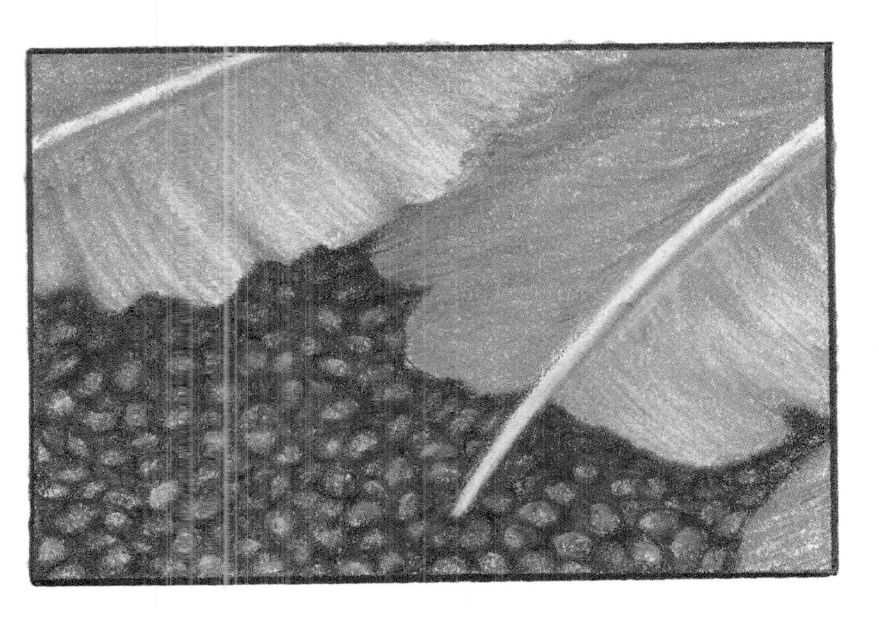

In box fermentation (used mostly in Asia) the beans are put into big wooden boxes with holes in the bottom so liquid from the pulp and the beans can run away. The boxes can hold up to two tonnes of beans, and the biggest are a metre deep. The beans are tipped from one box to another every day to make sure that they all get the same amount of air and drainage.

Which method makes the best chocolate? It depends on the beans and on the size of the heap or box. The smaller the heap or the box, the better the flavour ... but it's more work, so is more expensive for the farmers. Some tasters say box fermentation makes for a more bitter-tasting chocolate, but it depends who you ask.

4. DRYING. If the beans aren't properly dried after fermentation they go mouldy. If mouldy beans do slip through, whole batches of chocolate can be ruined; the taste is really horrible. On the other hand, if the beans are dried *too* much they get very brittle and are difficult to use. Ideally they should keep about seven to eight per cent of their original moisture. (Which isn't much. Pour out a glass of water and then take away 92 per cent and see what you're left with.)

Usually beans are dried in the sun on mats, trays or tables. They have to be protected at night and when it rains, so sometimes the tables are on wheels and can be hurried under cover if the clouds come up. On the other hand, sometimes the roof is on wheels! The beans are left for about a week and raked over.

5. STORAGE. It's important that the stored beans don't get wet. If they do, they go mouldy. But they also need air, so they are usually packed into sacks made of jute, a natural fibre that's strong and allows lots of ventilation. Once the beans are safely in their sacks, great care has to be taken not to store them near anything with a strong smell, or they take on an extra flavour – not everyone likes mustard-flavoured chocolate!

6. SHIPPING. Most beans are transported by ship. There is often condensation when the temperature drops as the ships sail off to the chilly North (or the chilly South) and if it gets into the sacks that means MOULD. So good ventilation is really important: lots of fresh air circulating means healthy beans.

Some cocoa-growing countries have begun processing the beans themselves. They get as far as producing COCOA LIQUOR, because it's easier to transport – no worries about damp and mould.

The shells are got rid of before shipping, and as these are only going to be thrown away anyway, that saves on costs too.

7. CLEANING. Once the beans reach the factory, the first stage is to make sure they're clean – after all, they've been dried on mats or tables, or sometimes in heaps under leaves. So they are shaken, sieved and brushed, and often giant vacuum cleaners are used to suck away dirt.

8. ROASTING. The beans are roasted to bring out what is called the AROMA. This is partly smell, but roasting changes the taste too. It also loosens the outer husk, so that it can be taken off in the next stage. Conveyor belts carry the beans through the heat, and they are roasted for 15–20 minutes.

9. CRUSHING and SHELLING. When the beans are crushed, the husks fall off, and because the husks are lighter than the beans, currents of air can be used to float them away. It's at this stage that the beans are blended – ten per cent Criollo beans might be mixed with 90 per cent Forastero, for example – but it all depends on what you want the end result to be.

10. GRINDING. Next the beans are ground into a paste. The action of grinding makes the cocoa butter in the beans melt, and the result is a thick, dark brown liquid, which sets again as it cools. Note: This is called cocoa liquor and it's the point at which the Maya and the Aztecs stopped – they used this paste as the basis for the chocolate they drank. It would have been very fatty, as none of the cocoa butter had been taken out: try making yourself a mug of hot chocolate, and then adding a large spoonful of butter. Nice?

11. PRESSING. Half the cocoa paste is put aside and will be used later. The rest is squished and squeezed by hydraulic presses until COCOA BUTTER flows out. This, once it's filtered and purified, is important in making the chocolate smooth and shiny, with that melt-in-the-mouth quality.

12. MIXING. The cocoa butter now meets up again with the unpressed cocoa paste, because chocolate is made from COCOA PASTE + SUGAR + COCOA BUTTER. (There isn't enough cocoa butter in one lot of pure chocolate paste to make lovely smooth chocolate ... it needs an extra helping.)

Milk chocolate is made from COCOA PASTE + SUGAR + COCOA BUTTER + MILK and white chocolate is COCOA BUTTER + SUGAR + MILK – it doesn't actually have any cocoa in it at all. (Incidentally, white chocolate is much harder to keep, which is why you'll always find it wrapped in foil.)

13. KNEADING, ROLLING and CONCHING. The different ingredients (depending on whether you're aiming for plain, milk or white chocolate) are kneaded together in a mixer, then put through rollers. But if you tasted the chocolate mixture at this stage it would still be slightly gritty and a little bitter, without any of the mellow smoothness you'd expect. It needs one final stage – conching.

The paste is heated and slapped to and fro by rollers for at least seventy-two hours, and this results in the taste and texture that we know and love.

14. FINALLY ... TEMPERING. The chocolate paste is heated to 50 °C, and then cooled down to 30 °C. This makes it thicker, and the right consistency for filling moulds. It also keeps the chocolate shiny and stops it developing a dull, grey bloom. (Have you ever left chocolate for a long time? If you have, you'll know that it tastes OK but looks very odd.)

If the chocolate isn't going to be used straight away, it is cooled into huge hundred-weight blocks or smaller sizes. Thousands of firms buy chocolate in this form to make their own particular bunnies or peppermint creams or whatever; but they don't ask for a block of chocolate – they ask for COUVERTURE which is the posh name for it!

Filled chocolates are made by creating a chocolate half-shell. The filling is then added and topped with more chocolate to seal it in – if you look at machine-made chocolates it's usually quite easy to spot the joining line. Hand-made chocolates are finished with more care, although sometimes the hand-making bit consists of nothing more than popping a sugared flower on the top.

If the chocolate is going to be made into a solid bar, machines pour the melted paste into moulds on a conveyor belt. The moulds are shaken to get rid of air bubbles and then cooled until the chocolate is solid enough to be turned out. Another conveyor belt takes the bars away to the wrapping machines ... and cardboard boxes ... and ships ... and lorries ... and shops.

The ideal temperature to store chocolate confectionary is 19–21°C. If it gets any warmer, we all know what happens – it melts. Indeed, one of the main reasons people love chocolate is that it melts at body heat. A slab is hard when you break a piece off, and the *snap!* is an important part of the whole experience. (There are experts whose job is to find the perfect snapping point of chocolate!) But once the snap has taken place and the piece is put in your mouth, it gradually dissolves, filling your mouth with soft smooth velvety sweetness...

Which is kind of where I started – eating chocolate and enjoying it. But there are still a few other things that you should know.

A FAIR DEAL FOR ALL

Over the last few years there has been much more interest in "real" chocolate. Specialist shops are springing up everywhere that offer a much higher cocoa content. Look out for them! It's become fashionable to like this stronger, less sweet chocolate – there are lots of claims for its health-giving properties, and new discoveries are being made all the time.

Are they true? Well ... sort of. Cocoa contains phenylethylamine, or PEA. This chemical is found in the brain and increases your heart rate and raises your blood pressure ... which isn't good for you. On the other hand, these are the symptoms you have when you're in love, so chocolate makes you feel good, even if it isn't doing you good.

Some scientists claim that chocolate stimulates the release of endorphins (chemicals produced in the brain) into the body. Endorphins make you feel happy – but exercise provides the same effect without the calories. (Of course, some people prefer eating chocolate to going on a five-mile walk.) There are antioxidants in cocoa too, which are excellent – but any benefits these might bring are cancelled out by sugar and fat.

World consumption of cocoa (excluding China, India and Indonesia, where very little chocolate is eaten) was an incredible 0.967 kg per head in 2001. If you want to check on the most recent statistics, look them up on **www.icco.org** – that's the International Cocoa Organization, and they have all the most recent trade figures. And remember that's the cocoa consumption – not the amount of chocolate eaten, with all its added fats and sugars. In the UK alone more than ten kilos of chocolate is eaten per person per year!

Ten kilos is an awful lot of chocolate.

And sugar.

And fat.

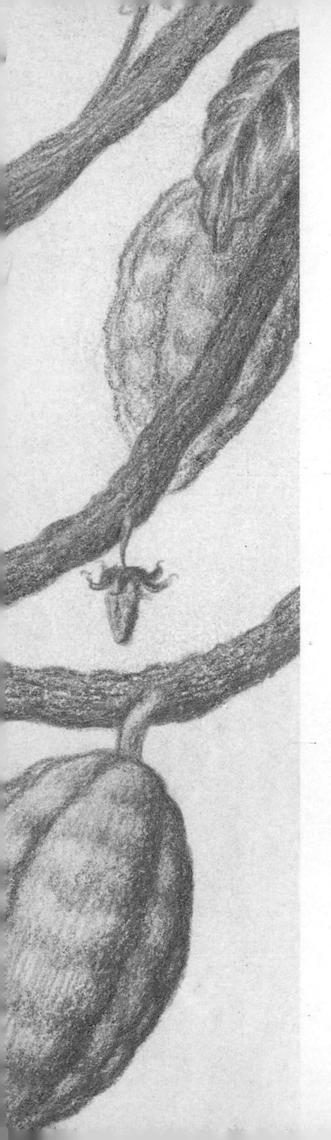

Now, I've learned a lot while researching this book, and one of the things that has really struck me is the obscene conditions in which some of the people who work on the cocoa plantations are forced to live. And we're talking NOW – not the seventeenth century. It's as near to slave labour as you can get. Huge amounts of herbicide and pesticide are sprayed on cocoa trees, endangering the lives of the workers, and presumably being taken up by the trees as well. And although chocolate is one of the most common foodstuffs in Europe and the US and Australasia, it's not available to the thousands and thousands and thousands of workers who grow, tend and harvest the beans. Many of these workers live at bare subsistence level; the collapse of just one year's cocoa crop is disastrous and means starvation ... while the end product is a luxury item for the other half of the world.

Some chocolate manufacturers are out to make as much money as they can, so they don't invest in health and insurance schemes for the chocolate farmers. If one crop fails, they move on to buy from another area where the beans are available ... and as you now know, cocoa trees are notoriously difficult to grow. A whole crop of beans can be wiped out by disease or bad weather, or just because the trees have decided have a year off, and the earnings of a whole community will vanish completely. Children won't be able to go to school, or be treated for illness – or even eat.

If you want to help this situation, look out for FAIRTRADE chocolate, such as the chocolate made by Green and Black, Divine and Traidcraft. The workers who produce the beans they use are better supported and have a reasonable deal with the buyers.

(If any other chocolate manufacturers read this and want to let me know how respectable their business practices are, I'd be delighted to hear. I'll put their names in the next edition ... IF they treat their suppliers fairly and with respect.)

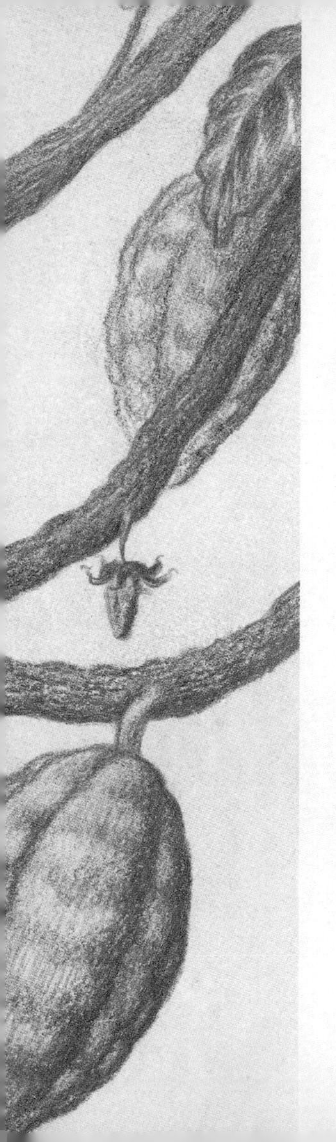

So I've made myself a promise about the sort of chocolate I buy. It has to be Fairtrade chocolate. It means that I'll be supporting cocoa plantations that treat their workers with a reasonable degree of decency and fairness. And anyway, it tastes good.
TRY SOME! See what you think. And think about where that chocolate has come from. Where those beans were grown. Maybe, just maybe, they came from a tree that grows on a patch of earth where *Theobroma cacao* trees have grown for thousands of years ... where a child once complained that she was thirsty, and her brother told her, "Suck the pulp, but spit out the seeds!"

THEOBROMA CACAO. FOOD OF THE GODS.

INDEX

Books I found fun to read, as well as enormously informative, were 'Indulgence' by Paul Richardson and 'The True History of Chocolate' by Sophie D. Coe and Michael D. Coe. There are many many MANY other books on chocolate, and I read an awful lot of them, and looked at literally hundreds of websites. Some were good, some were very technical, some were misleading, but I owe them all a huge debt of thanks. **V.F.**

3 8002 01864 7315

Chocolate/Food